(REMEMBER TO EXPLAIN YOUR ANSWERS!)

Would you rather share the same bathwater with your whole family for a week OR share a hot tub with a monkey for a night?

LAUGH POINT____/1

Would you rather have to use a shampoo made of snail slime OR body wash made of llama spit?

LAUGH POINT____/1

PLAYER 1

(REMEMBER TO EXPLAIN YOUR ANSWERS!)

Would you rather walk on a floor made of spiders OR sleep in a bed of spider webbing?

LAUGH POINT_____/1

Would you rather have to eat someone else's used tissues OR drink someone else's sweat?

LAUGH POINT_____/1

PLAYER 1

(REMEMBER TO EXPLAIN YOUR ANSWERS!)

Would you rather get stuck in a closet filled with snakes OR in a mud pit filled with worms, and you would have to dig your way out?

LAUGH POINT____/1

Would you rather sleep on a mattress covered in bedbugs OR use a blanket riddled with fleas?

LAUGH POINT____/1

PLAYER 1

(REMEMBER TO EXPLAIN YOUR ANSWERS!)

Would you rather share a tent with a woodpecker for a night OR share a bed with a drooling bulldog for a week?

LAUGH POINT____/1

Would you rather wear shoes filled with ants for a day OR wear a hat filled with slugs for a week?

LAUGH POINT____/1

PASS THE BOOK TO PLAYER 2

PLAYER 2

Would you rather have to bathe your cat with your tongue OR pick up dog poop with your bare feet?

LAUGH POINT_____/1

Would you rather use gooey snot as a hair gel to style your hair OR use frog mucous as hand cream?

LAUGH POINT_____/1

PLAYER 2

Would you rather walk like a penguin OR smell like a pig pen?

LAUGH POINT____/1

Would you rather have whiskers like a cat OR eyes of a fish that can't blink?

LAUGH POINT____/1

PLAYER 2

(REMEMBER TO EXPLAIN YOUR ANSWERS!)

Would you rather have toadstools grow out of your ears OR have a fir tree growing out of your nose?

LAUGH POINT_____/1

Would you rather eat a tablespoon of someone else's boogers OR a tablespoon of liquid soap?

LAUGH POINT_____/1

PLAYER 2

Would you rather have dandelions grow out of your head OR grass growing on your face like a beard?

LAUGH POINT___/1

Would you rather have beady eyes like a little bird OR have giant ears like an elephant?

LAUGH POINT___/1

PLAYER 1 _____ /8
ROUND TOTAL

PLAYER 2 _____ /8
ROUND TOTAL

ROUND CHAMPION!

PLAYER 1

(REMEMBER TO EXPLAIN YOUR ANSWERS!)

Would you rather have to wear your brother's smelly gym clothes for a week OR your grandma's perfume for a month?

LAUGH POINT____/1

Would you rather sleep on a park bench for a month OR in a graveyard for a week?

LAUGH POINT____/1

Would you rather wake up in a bird's nest as a tiny baby bird OR in a bat cave as a baby bat?

LAUGH POINT____/1

Would you rather have your classroom smell like fish guts for a week OR your bedroom smell like a stinky armpit for a month?

LAUGH POINT____/1

PLAYER 1

(REMEMBER TO EXPLAIN YOUR ANSWERS!)

Would you rather build a sculpture out of cow manure with your bare hands OR make a craft necklace using rotted donkey teeth?

LAUGH POINT____/1

Would you rather have a long, quick tongue like a frog to get your food OR have a mighty jaw like a crocodile to demolish your meals?

LAUGH POINT____/1

PLAYER 1

(REMEMBER TO EXPLAIN YOUR ANSWERS!)

Would you rather fly in an airplane filled with noisy seagulls OR sail in a rowboat filled with smelly, dead fishes?

LAUGH POINT____/1

Would you rather brush your teeth with toilet water OR wash your hair with dog saliva?

LAUGH POINT____/1

PASS THE BOOK TO PLAYER 2

PLAYER 2

(REMEMBER TO EXPLAIN YOUR ANSWERS!)

Would you rather have a bath in rice pudding OR a shower in iced tea?

 LAUGH POINT____/1

Would you rather have cotton-candy hair OR chocolate chip freckles?

 LAUGH POINT____/1

PLAYER 2

(REMEMBER TO EXPLAIN YOUR ANSWERS!)

Would you rather eat a tin of cat food OR a bowl of rotten pumpkin?

LAUGH POINT_____/1

Would you rather feed the lions at the zoo OR the sharks at the aquarium from your palm?

LAUGH POINT_____/1

PLAYER 2

(REMEMBER TO EXPLAIN YOUR ANSWERS!)

Would you rather lick the shoes of everyone in your family OR kiss a stranger's pet on the mouth?

LAUGH POINT____/1

Would you rather suck on a sour lemon for an hour OR drink a small bottle of hot sauce as fast as you can?

LAUGH POINT____/1

PLAYER 2

Would you rather have a bath in raw eggs OR take a swim in a tomato juice pool?

LAUGH POINT____/1

Would you rather have horns like a mountain goat OR hooves like a horse?

LAUGH POINT____/1

PLAYER 1  /8
ROUND TOTAL

PLAYER 2  /8
ROUND TOTAL

ROUND CHAMPION!

ROUND 3

PLAYER 1

Would you rather use chocolate pudding as a moisturizer OR use a cow patty as shampoo?

LAUGH POINT____/1

Would you rather fly a kite wearing pajamas in a snowstorm OR walk your dog wearing a swimsuit in a hailstorm?

LAUGH POINT____/1

PLAYER 1

(REMEMBER TO EXPLAIN YOUR ANSWERS!)

Would you rather wear mittens made of dog hair OR wear a scarf made of straw?

LAUGH POINT____/1

Would you rather play patty-cake with a grizzly bear OR play hide-and-go-seek with a skunk?

LAUGH POINT____/1

PLAYER 1

Would you rather take ballroom dancing lessons with a witch OR learn how to juggle with an old pirate who can't see too well?

LAUGH POINT____/1

Would you rather have to peel bubble gum off the sidewalk using only your teeth OR shovel cow manure all day in the middle of July?

LAUGH POINT____/1

PLAYER 1

Would you rather get caught in the rain made from frog spit OR snow made from frozen boogers?

LAUGH POINT____/1

Would you rather drink a smoothie made of salty dill pickles OR a hot tea made with armpit sweat?

LAUGH POINT____/1

PASS THE BOOK TO PLAYER 2

PLAYER 2

(REMEMBER TO EXPLAIN YOUR ANSWERS!)

Would you rather be able to lay eggs OR be the one to keep eggs warm with your body heat until they hatch?

LAUGH POINT____/1

Would you rather clean your family's dirty dishes using only your tongue OR scrub all the toilets with your bare hands?

LAUGH POINT____/1

PLAYER 2

Would you rather sleep on pillows made of marshmallows OR have blankets made of cotton candy?

LAUGH POINT____/1

Would you rather be stuck in a tent filled with mosquitoes for an hour OR in a hotel room filled with bedbugs for a night?

LAUGH POINT____/1

PLAYER 2

(REMEMBER TO EXPLAIN YOUR ANSWERS!)

Would you rather have your only snacks be dog treats OR drink your drinks from the dog's bowl?

LAUGH POINT____/1

Would you rather have leeches on your skin for a day OR leave your hand in a beehive for an hour?

LAUGH POINT____/1

PLAYER 2

Would you rather take a trip to the moon with a chimpanzee OR go deep-sea diving with an octopus?

LAUGH POINT____/1

Would you rather eat a live beetle you could dip in chocolate OR a tablespoon of dead ants?

LAUGH POINT____/1

PLAYER 1 _____ /8

ROUND TOTAL

PLAYER 2 _____ /8

ROUND TOTAL

_____

ROUND CHAMPION!

Would you rather win the world record for the largest ears OR the biggest nose?

LAUGH POINT____/1

Would you rather have your school desk filled with moldy cheese OR your locker filled with cockroaches?

LAUGH POINT____/1

PLAYER 1

Would you rather play pool with rotten eggs OR play darts with sharpened chicken bones?

LAUGH POINT_____/1

Would you rather eat five giant grasshoppers OR twenty bumblebees?

LAUGH POINT_____/1

PLAYER 1

Would you rather set sail on an ocean made of dirty, old dishwater OR on a river made of runny snot?

LAUGH POINT____/1

Would you rather play leapfrog with a porcupine OR hopscotch with a warthog?

LAUGH POINT____/1

PLAYER 1

Would you rather eat a bunch of dandelions covered in ranch dressing OR eat a mud pie topped with pine needles?

LAUGH POINT____/1

Would you rather climb a cactus in your underwear OR sleep in a pine tree for a night?

LAUGH POINT____/1

PASS THE BOOK TO PLAYER 2

PLAYER 2

(REMEMBER TO EXPLAIN YOUR ANSWERS!)

Would you rather eat a cup of dead flies OR two live worms?

LAUGH POINT____/1

Would you rather have a horn like a rhinoceros OR a neck like a giraffe?

LAUGH POINT____/1

PLAYER 2

(REMEMBER TO EXPLAIN YOUR ANSWERS!)

Would you rather prefer you always had an itchy butt OR a sore throat?

 LAUGH POINT____/1

Would you rather have to pee every time it rains OR sneeze every time it snows?

 LAUGH POINT____/1

PLAYER 2

Would you rather eat your way out of a giant bowl of raw mushrooms OR have to smell rotten mushrooms for a month?

LAUGH POINT____/1

Would you rather slide down a waterslide made of mustard OR swim in a wave pool with jellyfish?

LAUGH POINT____/1

PLAYER 2

Would you rather sweep the whole house using your bare hands OR carry the garbage out using your teeth?

LAUGH POINT_____/1

Would you rather prefer your nose was located where your belly button is, OR your mouth was down by your ankles?

LAUGH POINT_____/1

PLAYER 1

_____ /8

ROUND TOTAL

PLAYER 2

_____ /8

ROUND TOTAL

_____

ROUND CHAMPION!

ROUND 5

PLAYER 1

Would you rather win the record for the sharpest, most prolonged teeth OR for bushiest eyebrows?

LAUGH POINT____/1

Would you rather quack like a duck and live in a pond OR meow like a cat and live at the dumpsite?

LAUGH POINT____/1

PLAYER 1

(REMEMBER TO EXPLAIN YOUR ANSWERS!)

Would you rather sweat ketchup out of your armpits OR have lime Kool-Aid as saliva?

LAUGH POINT____/1

Would you rather have five eyes like bee OR have a stinger like a wasp?

LAUGH POINT____/1

Would you rather prefer that the sidewalks were made of quicksand, but you were the fastest runner in the world, OR the streets were covered in water, but you had duck feet?

LAUGH POINT____/1

Would you rather prefer that rain was made of mustard OR snow was made of pistachio ice cream with salt?

LAUGH POINT____/1

(REMEMBER TO EXPLAIN YOUR ANSWERS!)

Would you rather be stuck on a roller coaster with a nauseous hyena OR take a road trip with a flatulent gorilla?

LAUGH POINT____/1

Would you rather have your eyelids glued shut, OR your mouth taped closed for a whole day at school?

LAUGH POINT____/1

PASS THE BOOK TO PLAYER 2

PLAYER 2

(REMEMBER TO EXPLAIN YOUR ANSWERS!)

Would you rather like that you always had the smell of cat pee on your clothes OR the scent of garlic sauce in your hair?

LAUGH POINT____/1

Would you rather have to always blow your nose with your T-shirt OR have to always wipe your sweat with your underwear?

LAUGH POINT____/1

PLAYER 2

Would you rather sleep in a beaver dam for a night OR beneath a wasp's nest for a week?

LAUGH POINT_____/1

Would you rather pick olives off of olive trees with only your teeth OR climb palm trees wearing your underwear and a monkey mask?

LAUGH POINT_____/1

PLAYER 2

(REMEMBER TO EXPLAIN YOUR ANSWERS!)

Would you rather croak like a raven every Friday OR sing everything you say on Sundays?

LAUGH POINT____/1

Would you rather bite someone else's toenails OR have your fingernails sprinkled on your birthday cake?

LAUGH POINT____/1
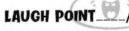

PLAYER 2

Would you rather live in a houseboat with a hippopotamus OR in a cave with a leopard?

LAUGH POINT____/1

Would you rather wash your face with gasoline OR wash your hair with mayonnaise?

LAUGH POINT____/1

PLAYER 1 _____ /8
ROUND TOTAL

PLAYER 2 _____ /8
ROUND TOTAL

ROUND CHAMPION!

PLAYER 1

Would you rather get stranded in a jungle with no map OR get stuck in the attic of your own house, but no one can hear you?

LAUGH POINT____/1

Would you rather drink a banana milkshake made with the peels OR eat only unripe strawberries for a day?

LAUGH POINT____/1

PLAYER 1

Would you rather have a garden that grew gnomes OR a flower that was home to fairies?

LAUGH POINT____/1

Would you rather tame a tiger in a circus OR be stuck in a clown's car with ten other clowns?

LAUGH POINT____/1

PLAYER 1

(REMEMBER TO EXPLAIN YOUR ANSWERS!)

Would you rather have to ride a spitting llama to school every day OR take a bus filled with birds who won't stop tweeting?

LAUGH POINT_____/1

Would you rather have morning breath all day long for a year OR smell like rotten eggs for a month?

LAUGH POINT_____/1

PLAYER 1

(REMEMBER TO EXPLAIN YOUR ANSWERS!)

Would you rather use toenail clippings as toothpicks OR your grandmother's hair as dental floss?

LAUGH POINT____/1

Would you rather have to constantly sneeze for a day OR burb constantly for a week?

LAUGH POINT____/1

PASS THE BOOK TO PLAYER 2

PLAYER 2

(REMEMBER TO EXPLAIN YOUR ANSWERS!)

Would you rather listen with your tongue and taste with your ears OR smell with your eyes and see with your nose?

LAUGH POINT____/1

Would you rather be forced to keep a dirty diaper in your locker for a week OR keep a moldy hamburger in your desk for a month?

LAUGH POINT____/1

PLAYER 2

(REMEMBER TO EXPLAIN YOUR ANSWERS!)

Would you rather have moths living in your mattress OR have caterpillars in your bathtub?

LAUGH POINT___/1

Would you rather prefer that you could only pick your nose with your big toe OR you could only scratch your skin with your teeth?

LAUGH POINT___/1

PLAYER 2

(REMEMBER TO EXPLAIN YOUR ANSWERS!)

Would you rather have all your food covered in earwax OR have all your drinks spiked with snot?

LAUGH POINT____/1

Would you rather have a homeless dog lick you clean as a bath OR have a homeless cat comb your hair with her paws?

LAUGH POINT____/1

PLAYER 2

(REMEMBER TO EXPLAIN YOUR ANSWERS!)

Would you rather stick your face in a bowl of spiders OR dip your foot in a bowl of crabs?

LAUGH POINT____/1

Would you rather sit on a cushion made of rose thorns OR have to run over burning, hot coals?

LAUGH POINT____/1

PLAYER 1

/8
ROUND TOTAL

PLAYER 2

/8
ROUND TOTAL

ROUND
CHAMPION!

ROUND 7

PLAYER 1

Would you rather live inside your favorite movie, but you are the character no one likes OR your favorite video game, but you keep dying over and over?

LAUGH POINT____/1

Would you rather eat a sandwich made by a mad doctor with any ingredients he chooses OR eat a sandwich made by a monkey with random four ingredients in the kitchen?

LAUGH POINT____/1

PLAYER 1

(REMEMBER TO EXPLAIN YOUR ANSWERS!)

Would you rather drink a potion that could turn you into the twin of someone you know OR drink a potion that could make you invisible for an hour?

LAUGH POINT_____/1

Would you rather ride inside a moldy pumpkin coach like a Cinderella with bad luck OR wear a spacesuit filled with spiders like a cursed Buzz Lightyear?

LAUGH POINT_____/1

PLAYER 1

Would you rather have ants come out from your mouth every time you sneeze OR worms every time you cough?

LAUGH POINT_____/1

Would you rather have a nose that grows when you lie OR have eyes that change color based on your moods?

LAUGH POINT_____/1

PLAYER 1

(REMEMBER TO EXPLAIN YOUR ANSWERS!)

Would you rather make a sculpture out of wet dog food OR paint a painting using different-colored snot?

LAUGH POINT____/1

Would you rather have to kiss your dad's stinky feet OR hug a prickly porcupine?

LAUGH POINT____/1

PASS THE BOOK TO PLAYER 2

PLAYER 2

Would you rather have tears that tasted like raw onions OR have sweat that was a bright, neon green?

LAUGH POINT_____/1

Would you rather get stuck hanging upside down in a roller coaster for ten minutes OR get stuck at the top of a giant Ferris wheel for a day?

LAUGH POINT_____/1

PLAYER 2

Would you rather slide down a waterslide made of olive juice OR drive a bumper car filled with month-old spaghetti sauce?

LAUGH POINT____/1

Would you rather have to clean out the fridge by eating everything that's left inside OR clean the bathroom sink using your tongue?

LAUGH POINT____/1

PLAYER 2

Would you rather use a bath towel made of sandpaper OR toilet paper made of velcro?

LAUGH POINT____/1

Would you rather have foot-long eyelashes OR never be able to grow hair on your head again?

LAUGH POINT____/1

PLAYER 2

Would you rather wear a shirt made of your sister's hair OR wear pants made of poison ivy?

LAUGH POINT____/1

Would you rather play a round of bowling with rotten melons OR tennis with spoiled peaches?

LAUGH POINT____/1

PLAYER 1 _____ /8
ROUND TOTAL

PLAYER 2 _____ /8

ROUND TOTAL

ROUND CHAMPION!

ROUND 8

PLAYER 1

(REMEMBER TO EXPLAIN YOUR ANSWERS!)

Would you rather have to wear roller skates permanently for a week OR snow boots for an entire summer?

LAUGH POINT____/1

Would you rather have teeth made out of hard candies OR hair made of Silly String?

LAUGH POINT____/1

PLAYER 1

Would you rather have your index finger be a fork OR your thumb be a spoon?

LAUGH POINT____/1

Would you rather have fish scales for skin OR a wagging dog's tail?

LAUGH POINT____/1

PLAYER 1

Would you rather have the rough, sandpapery tongue of a cat OR a bird's beak instead of a nose?

LAUGH POINT____/1

Would you rather drink expired orange juice for a month OR eat moldy ham and cheese sandwiches for a week?

LAUGH POINT____/1

PLAYER 1

Would you rather have fingernails made from sticky toffee OR toenails made from rotten banana peels?

LAUGH POINT____/1

Would you rather dig through a 10-foot pit of cow manure OR play in a sandbox filled with spiders?

LAUGH POINT____/1

PASS THE BOOK TO PLAYER 2

PLAYER 2

Would you rather be bitten by a rat OR take a bath with an electric ray?

LAUGH POINT____/1

Would you rather have baby hands OR baby feet?

LAUGH POINT____/1

PLAYER 2

(REMEMBER TO EXPLAIN YOUR ANSWERS!)

Would you rather paint your bedroom with bird poop OR use snakeskin as bedsheets?

LAUGH POINT____/1

Would you rather climb an old fir tree covered in Vaseline OR build a treehouse in a giant cactus?

LAUGH POINT____/1

PLAYER 2

Would you rather have ears made out of rotten mushrooms OR a skin made from bubble wrap?

LAUGH POINT____/1

Would you rather have to survive off of someone else's chewed bubble gum for a week OR mango and onions for a month?

LAUGH POINT____/1

PLAYER 2

Would you rather eat cake with seaweed icing and mud OR a pie filled with zucchini and grated golf balls?

LAUGH POINT____/1

Would you rather have a TV that lets you perceive every bad smell on the screen OR a tablet that amplifies every annoying noise a hundred times?

LAUGH POINT____/1

PLAYER 1 _____ /8
ROUND TOTAL

PLAYER 2 _____ /8
ROUND TOTAL

ROUND CHAMPION!

ROUND 9

PLAYER 1

(REMEMBER TO EXPLAIN YOUR ANSWERS!)

Would you rather burp every time you tell a secret OR sneeze every time you give a compliment?

LAUGH POINT _____/1

Would you rather have to cut and clean eighty fish in the blazing hot sun OR cook enough vegetable soup for eighty people at the North Pole?

LAUGH POINT _____/1

PLAYER 1

Would you rather muck horse stalls with your bare hands OR get pooped on by a flock of seagulls?

LAUGH POINT____/1

Would you rather have a dog's breath whenever you talk to someone you like OR smell like a sweaty armpit whenever you laugh?

LAUGH POINT____/1

PLAYER 1

(REMEMBER TO EXPLAIN YOUR ANSWERS!)

Would you rather have hot dog wieners for fingers OR hot dog buns for toes?

LAUGH POINT____/1

Would you rather have permanently sweaty palms OR a constantly runny nose?

LAUGH POINT____/1

PLAYER 1

Would you rather walk around covered in mud for a week OR go without a bath/shower for a month?

LAUGH POINT____/1

Would you rather wear a raccoon as a hat for a day OR share your room with a skunk for a week?

LAUGH POINT____/1

PASS THE BOOK TO PLAYER 2

PLAYER 2

(REMEMBER TO EXPLAIN YOUR ANSWERS!)

Would you rather shave your grandfather's hairy toes OR clean out your brother's ear wax?

LAUGH POINT____/1

Would you rather have a stomach that can talk and shout at you every time it's hungry OR have ears that secrete smelly vapor every time you overthink?

LAUGH POINT____/1

PLAYER 2

Would you rather eat cat food for breakfast every day for a year OR have sour milk in your cereal for the rest of your life?

LAUGH POINT____/1

Would you rather sleep in your school's bathroom for a night OR share a room with someone's snoring grandma for a month?

LAUGH POINT____/1

PLAYER 2

(REMEMBER TO EXPLAIN YOUR ANSWERS!)

Would you rather take a train filled with zoo animals across the country OR go on a day-long road trip with ten car-sick kids?

LAUGH POINT____/1

Would you rather take a shower where spiders come out of the showerhead OR take a bath in a tub filled with frogs?

LAUGH POINT____/1

PLAYER 2

Would you rather eat toast with a toenail jam spread OR a wrap filled with belly button lint?

LAUGH POINT____/1

Would you rather eat a frozen pizza off the sidewalk using only your mouth OR use a toothbrush that was dropped in the toilet?

LAUGH POINT____/1

PLAYER 1  **/8**

ROUND TOTAL

PLAYER 2 **/8**

ROUND TOTAL

ROUND CHAMPION!

PLAYER 1

Would you rather eat a pound of raw potato OR two pounds of raw apples with worms inside?

LAUGH POINT____/1

Would you rather wear sweaty gym socks as mittens all winter long OR a heavy sweater all summer?

LAUGH POINT____/1

PLAYER 1

Would you rather have tongues coming out of your ears OR extra eyes on your shoulders?

LAUGH POINT____/1

Would you rather have a chest made of armor OR a head made of steel?

LAUGH POINT____/1

PLAYER 1

Would you rather be transformed into your family's pet dog OR age ahead thirty years?

LAUGH POINT____/1

Would you rather have bubblegum always tasting like seaweed OR candy always tasting like dirt?

LAUGH POINT____/1

PLAYER 1

Would you rather be stuck in a locker room filled with sweaty sumo wrestlers OR in an elevator with your grandfather who just ate some bad clams?

LAUGH POINT____/1

Would you rather hike the rainforest on the back of a gorilla in the sweltering heat OR scale Mount Everest while riding a mountain goat?

LAUGH POINT____/1

PASS THE BOOK TO PLAYER 2

PLAYER 2

(REMEMBER TO EXPLAIN YOUR ANSWERS!)

Would you rather bark like a dog for a year instead of speaking OR burp through your entire school days?

LAUGH POINT____/1

Would you rather eat a bowl of your own hair with only ketchup to wash it down OR a tablespoon of snot with a glass of eggnog?

LAUGH POINT____/1

PLAYER 2

Would you rather climb a fence covered in thorny rose bushes OR a ladder covered in snot?

LAUGH POINT____/1

Would you rather be able to see like an eagle but also have talons for hands OR be able to smell like a hound dog but also have its tail and ears?

LAUGH POINT____/1

PLAYER 2

Would you rather mud puddles were made of chocolate pudding OR that rain was made of fruit punch?

LAUGH POINT____/1

Would you rather change poopy baby diapers every day for the rest of your life OR get pooped on by a pigeon every time you go outside?

LAUGH POINT____/1

PLAYER 2

Would you rather carry a bag of worms with you everywhere you go OR sleep on a bed of worms for a week?

LAUGH POINT____/1

Would you rather eat a dill pickle and broccoli ice cream shake OR a peanut butter and baked bean pear-walnut sandwich?

LAUGH POINT____/1

PLAYER 1 _____ /8
ROUND TOTAL

PLAYER 2 _____ /8
ROUND TOTAL

_____

ROUND CHAMPION!

ADD UP ALL YOUR POINTS FROM EACH ROUND.
THE PLAYER WITH THE MOST POINTS BECOMES
THE SUPER JOKESTER!

PLAYER 1 _____ /80
GRAND TOTAL

PLAYER 2 _____ /80
GRAND TOTAL

_____

 # THE SUPER JOKESTER!

TRY NOT TO LAUGH CHALLENGE

WOULD YOU RATHER?

EWW! EDITION

BOOK 2

COME UP WITH YOUR OWN HILARIOUS "WOULD YOU RATHER" JOKE. AND POSSIBLY IT WILL BE PUBLISHED IN OUR NEW BOOK!

SEND YOUR JOKES TO

COOLACTIVITYBOOKS@GMAIL.COM

WELCOME TO
WOULD YOU RATHER? EWW EDITION
HERE ARE THE RULES OF THE GAME:

- **PLAYER 1 READS THE WOULD YOU RATHER QUESTION ALOUD.**

- **PLAYER 2 VOICES ONE OF TWO HILARIOUS CHOICES IN THE GOOFIEST WAY POSSIBLE.**

- **PLAYER 2 EXPLAINS 'WHY' THIS SCENARIO WAS PICKED!**

- **IF THE EXPLANATION GETS A LAUGH, PLAYER 2 GETS A LAUGH POINT.**

- **MARK LAUGH POINTS IN A SPECIAL BOX!**

- **TAKE TURNS AND CALCULATE WHO WILL GET MORE LAUGH POINTS AND BECOME THE SUPER JOKESTER!**

Made in the USA
Las Vegas, NV
27 November 2022